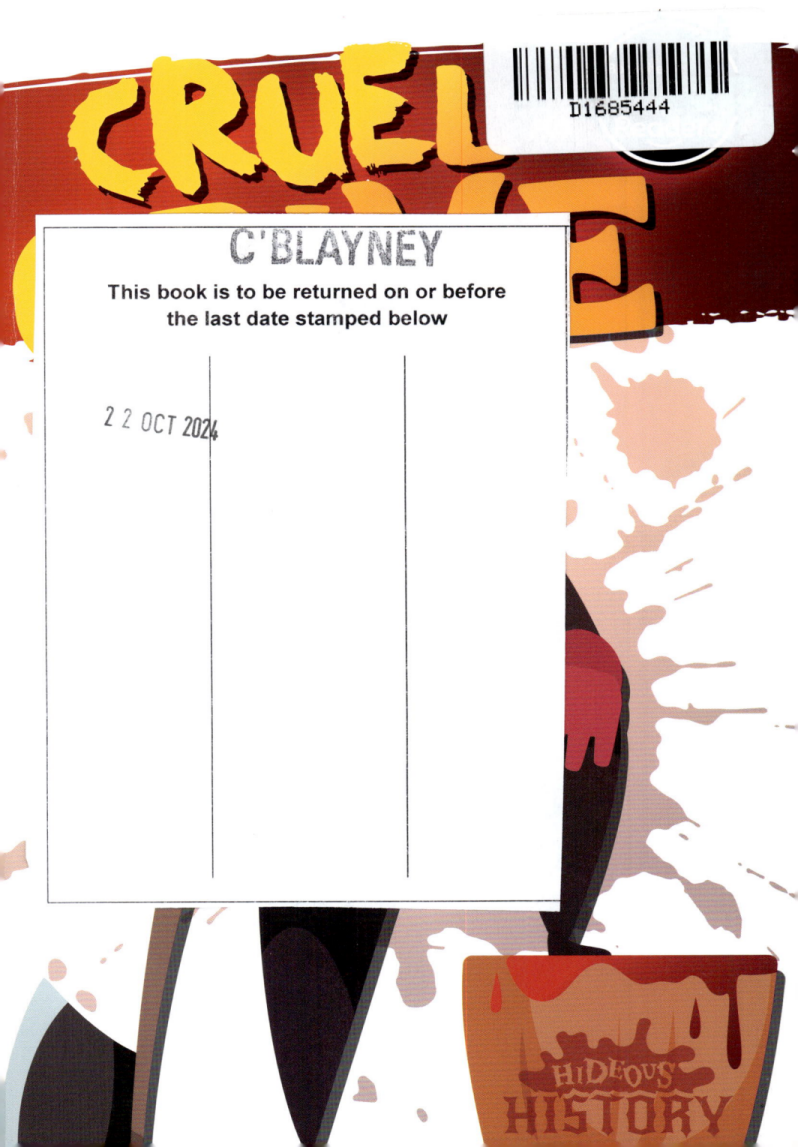

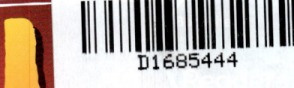

C'BLAYNEY

This book is to be returned on or before the last date stamped below

2 2 OCT 2024

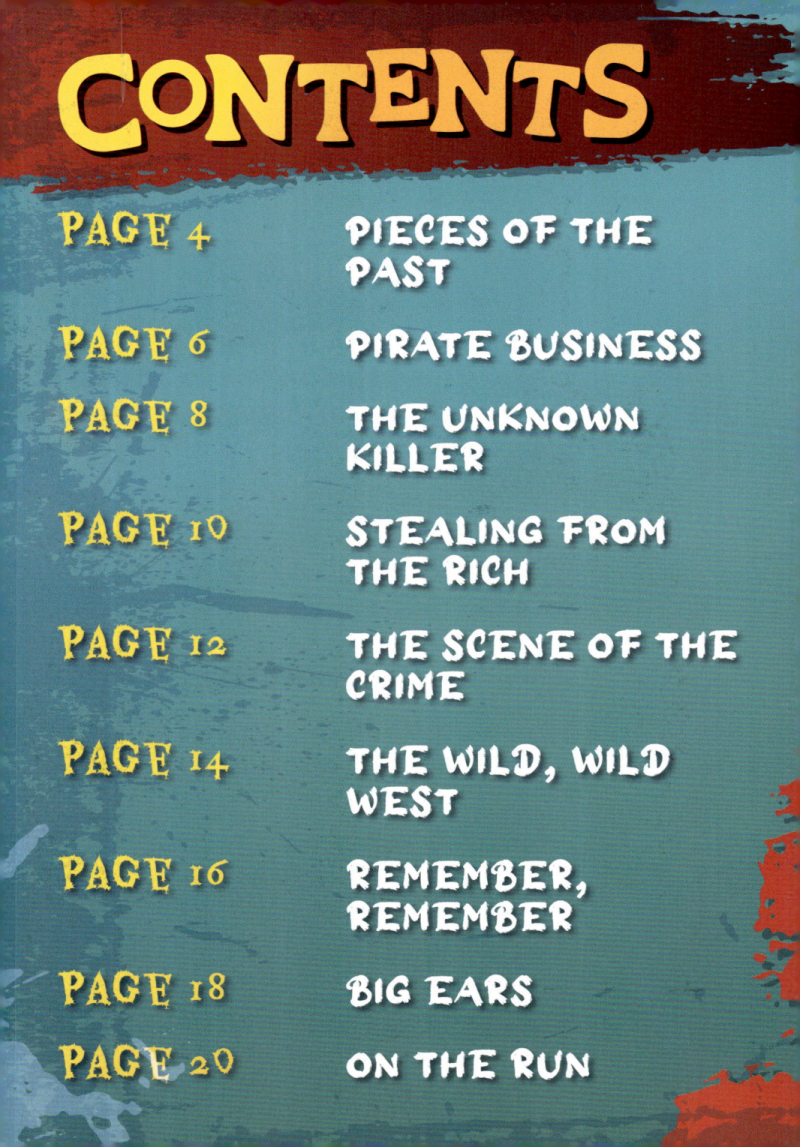

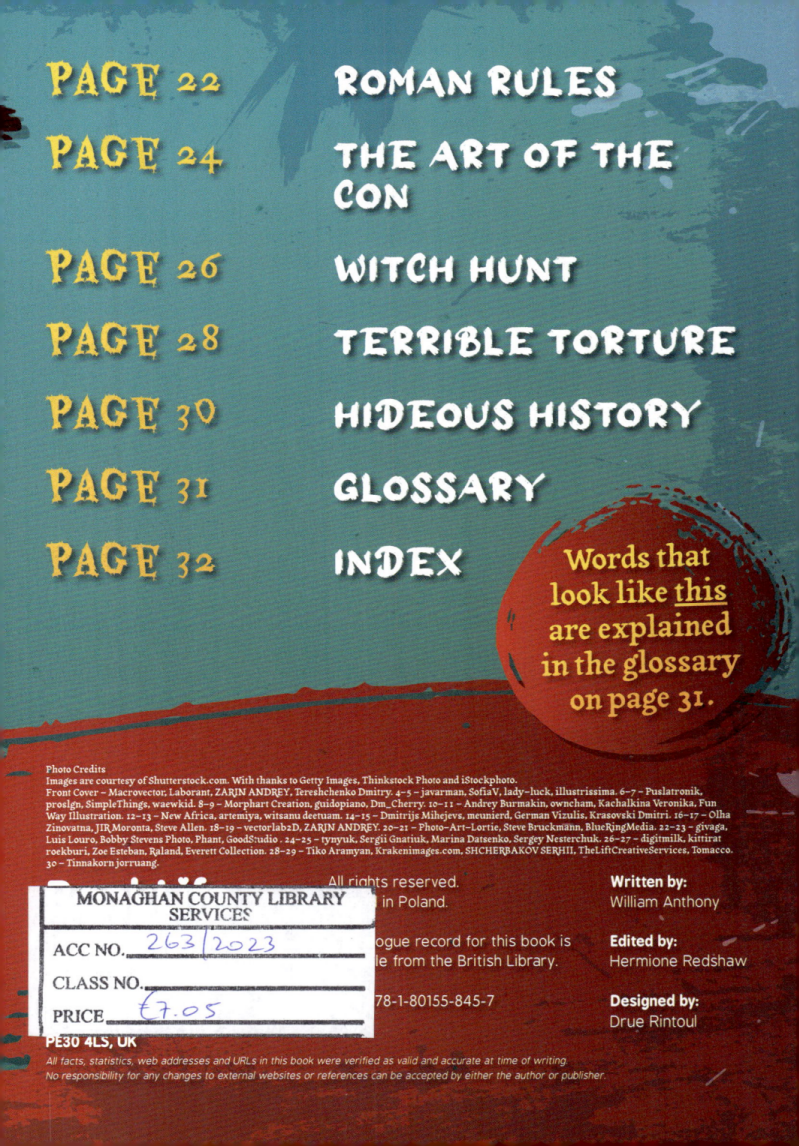

PAGE 22	**ROMAN RULES**
PAGE 24	**THE ART OF THE CON**
PAGE 26	**WITCH HUNT**
PAGE 28	**TERRIBLE TORTURE**
PAGE 30	**HIDEOUS HISTORY**
PAGE 31	**GLOSSARY**
PAGE 32	**INDEX**

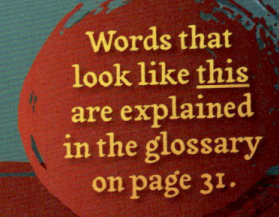

Words that look like this are explained in the glossary on page 31.

Photo Credits
Images are courtesy of Shutterstock.com. With thanks to Getty Images, Thinkstock Photo and iStockphoto.
Front Cover – Macrovector, Laborant, ZARJN ANDREY, Tereshchenko Dmitry. 4–5 – javarman, SofiaV, lady-luck, illustrissima. 6–7 – Puslatronik, proalgn, SimpleThings, waewkid. 8–9 – Morphart Creation, guidopiano, Dm_Cherry. 10–11 – Andrey Burmakin, owncham, Kachalkina Veronika, Fun Way Illustration. 12–13 – New Africa, artemiya, witsamu deetuum. 14–15 – Dmitrijs Mihejevs, meunlerd, German Vizulis, Krasovski Dmitri. 16–17 – Olha Zinovana, JTB,Morosita, Steve Allen. 18–19 – vectorlabsD, ZARJN ANDREY. 20–21 – Photo-Art-Lortie, Steve Bruckmann, BlueRingMedia. 22–23 – givaga, Luis Louro, Bobby Stevens Photo, Phant, GoodStudio. 24–25 – tinyuk, Sergii Gnatiuk, Marina Dutsenko, Sergey Nesterchunk. 26–27 – digitalis, kirtinet roekhart, Zoe Esteban, Raland, Everett Collection. 28–29 – Tiko Aramyan, Krakenimages.com, SHCHERBAKOV SERHII, TheLifeCreativeServices, Tomacco. 30 – Tinnakorn jorruang.

All rights reserved.
in Poland.

ogue record for this book is from the British Library.

78-1-80155-845-7

Written by:
William Anthony

Edited by:
Hermione Redshaw

Designed by:
Drue Rintoul

PE30 4LS, UK

All facts, statistics, web addresses and URLs in this book were verified as valid and accurate at time of writing.
No responsibility for any changes to external websites or references can be accepted by either the author or publisher.

PIECES OF THE PAST

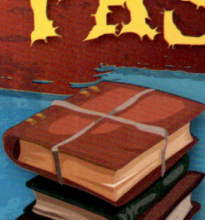

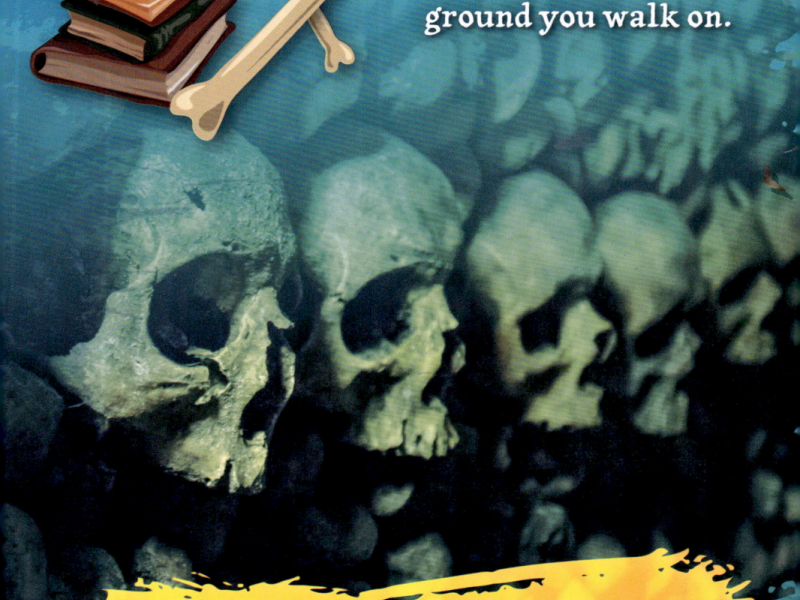

You can find secrets underground. You just have to know where to look. You can find bones, books, bodies and weapons under the ground you walk on.

The past was not kind to the people that lived through it. People didn't live very long, and it's no surprise as to why.

Disease and war were everywhere. People were punished for crimes they did not commit. No one was ever far from disaster, either. Yet, people still lived their lives.

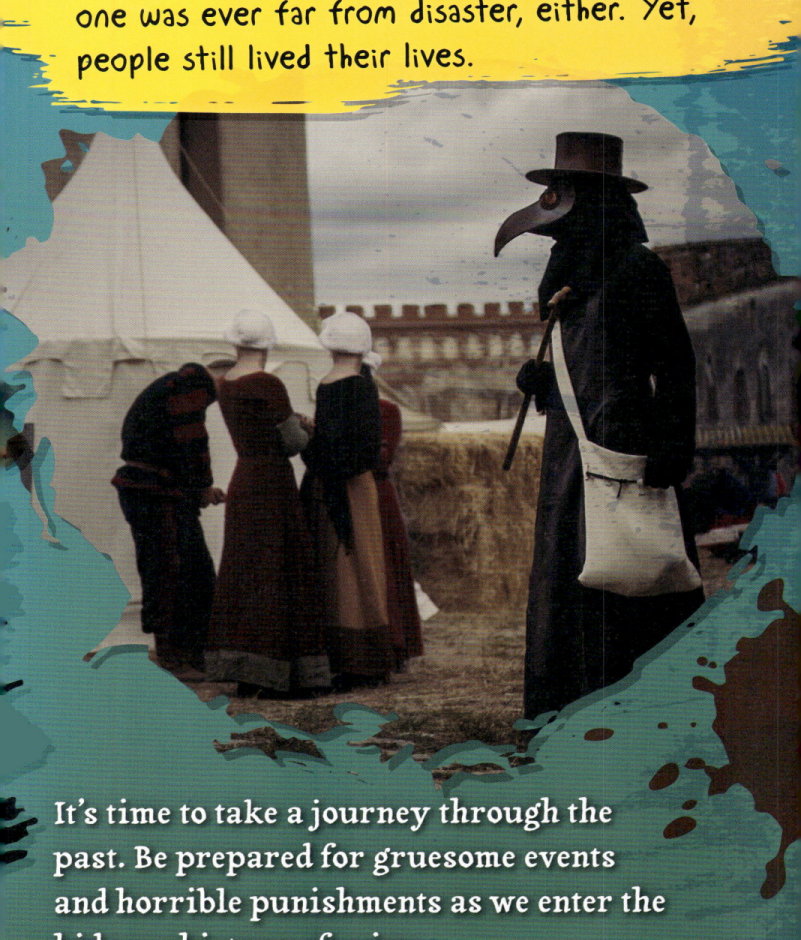

It's time to take a journey through the past. Be prepared for gruesome events and horrible punishments as we enter the hideous history of crime...

PIRATE BUSINESS

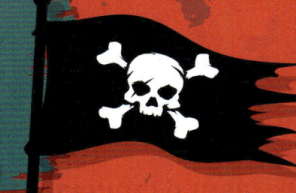

Have you ever heard of Blackbeard? What about Barbarossa? You probably think they are some of the most fearsome pirates of all time.

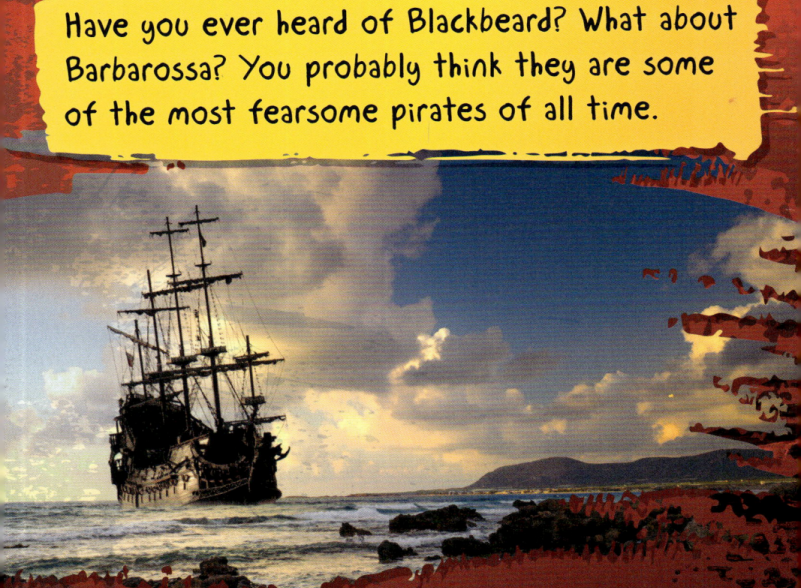

They were nothing compared to Ching Shih. She was one of the greatest pirates of all time. Historians believe she was born in China in 1775.

Ching Shih was the leader of a group of ships called The Red Flag Fleet. She took control of it when her husband died. The Red Flag Fleet went on to rob lots of towns and ships.

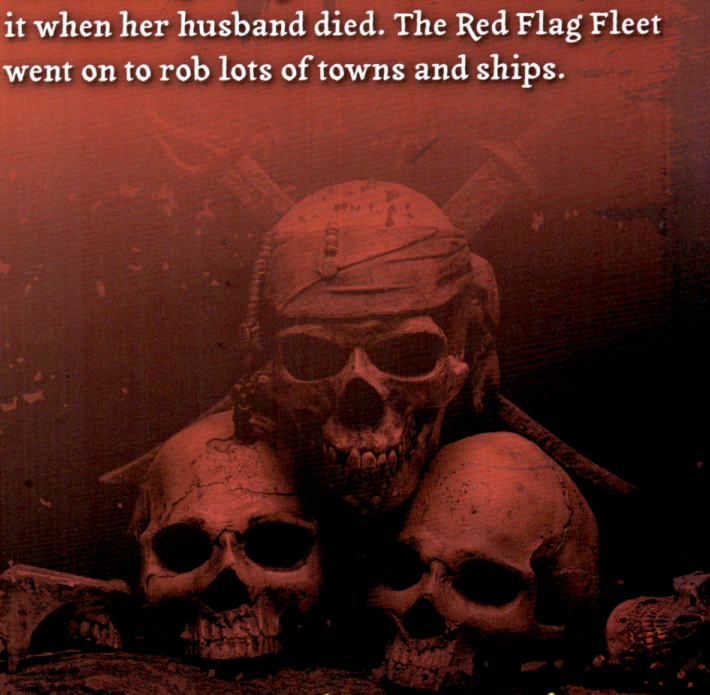

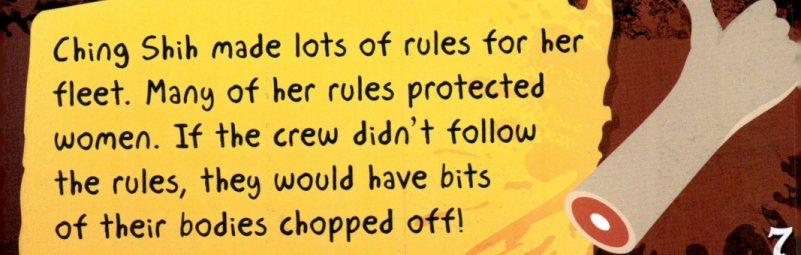

Ching Shih made lots of rules for her fleet. Many of her rules protected women. If the crew didn't follow the rules, they would have bits of their bodies chopped off!

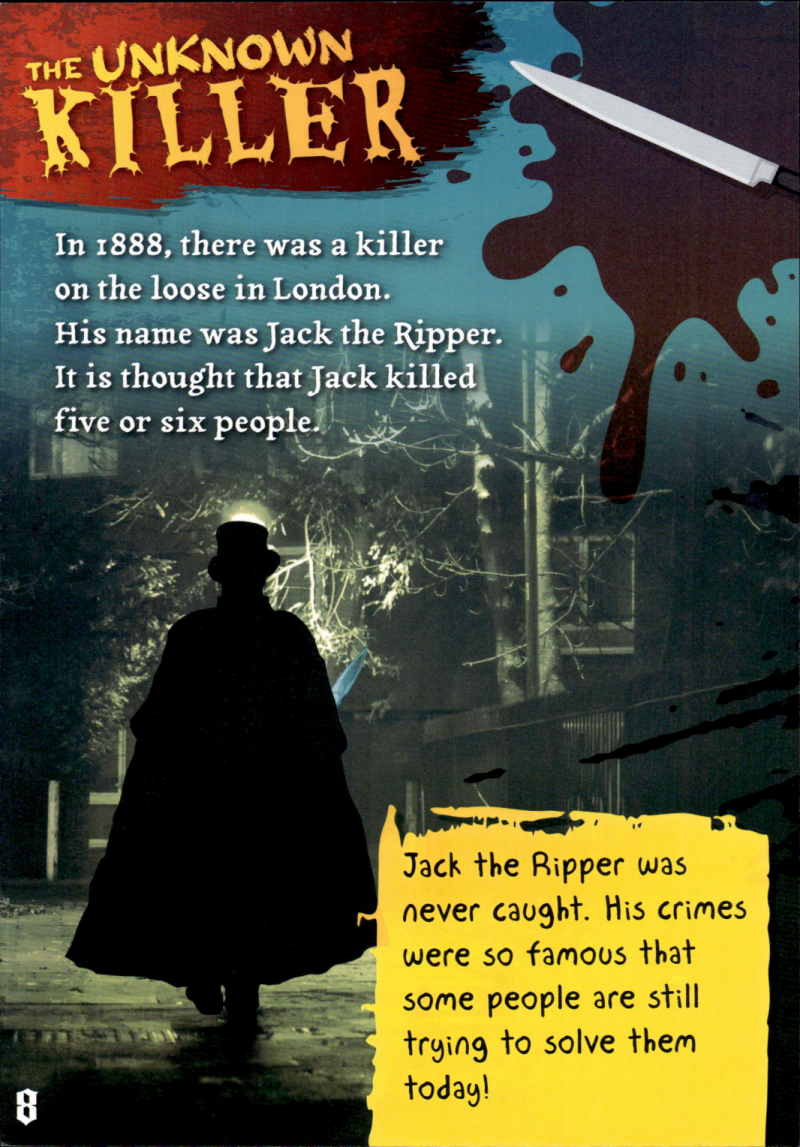

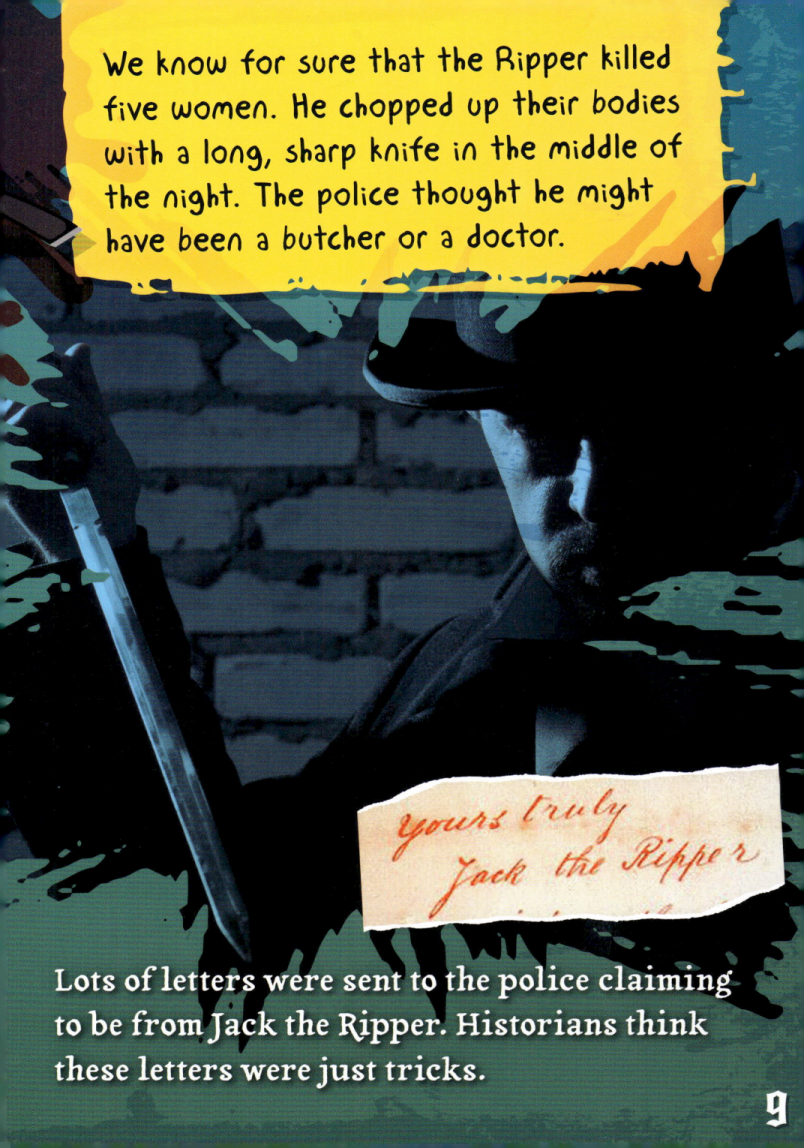

STEALING FROM THE RICH

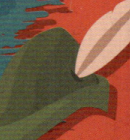

Robin Hood was an outlaw in England around the 12th century. He knew how to fight with a bow and arrow. He lived in Sherwood Forest with other outlaws called the Merry Men.

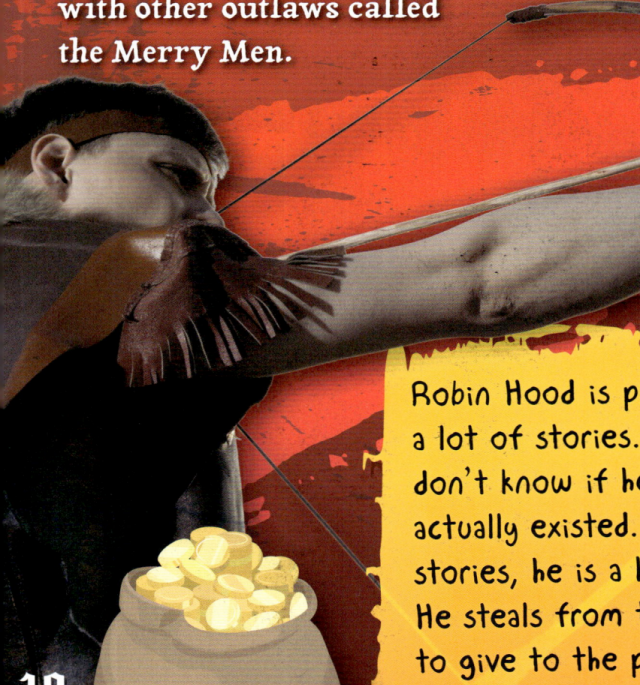

Robin Hood is part of a lot of stories. We don't know if he ever actually existed. In the stories, he is a hero. He steals from the rich to give to the poor.

Records show that outlaws often called themselves names that sounded like Robin Hood. People think this might be because of the story. Others think it is because he really existed.

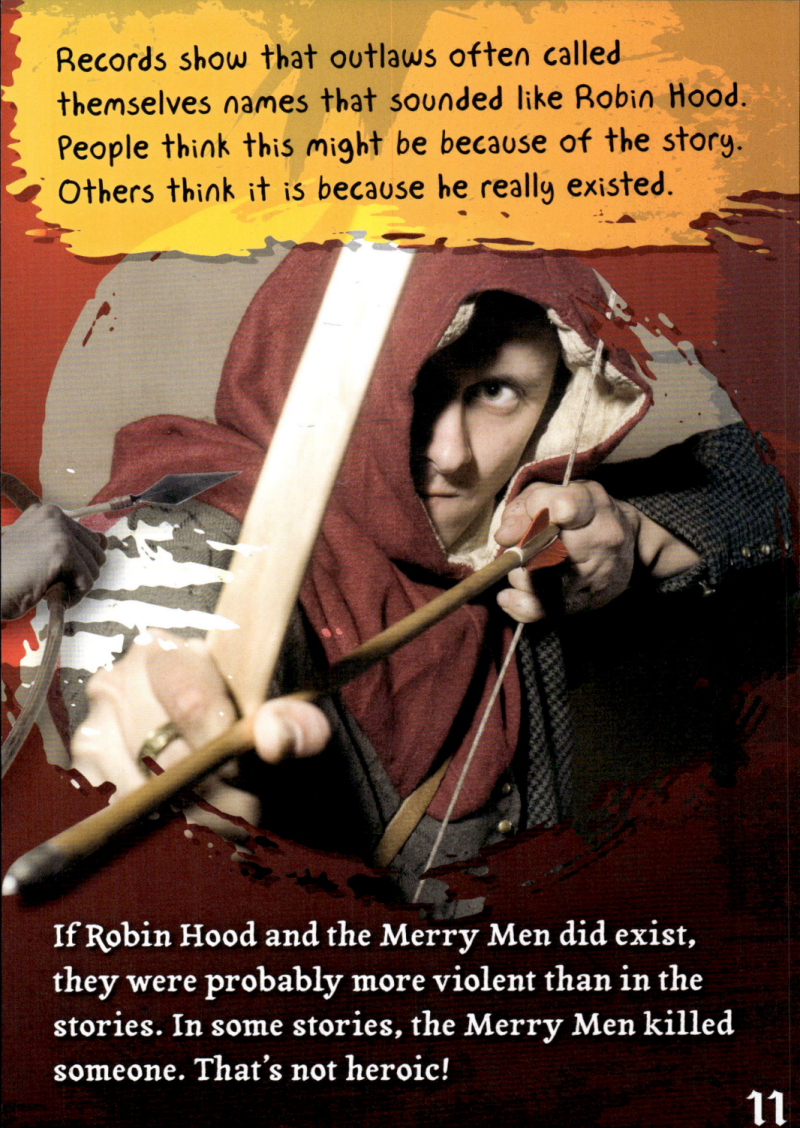

If Robin Hood and the Merry Men did exist, they were probably more violent than in the stories. In some stories, the Merry Men killed someone. That's not heroic!

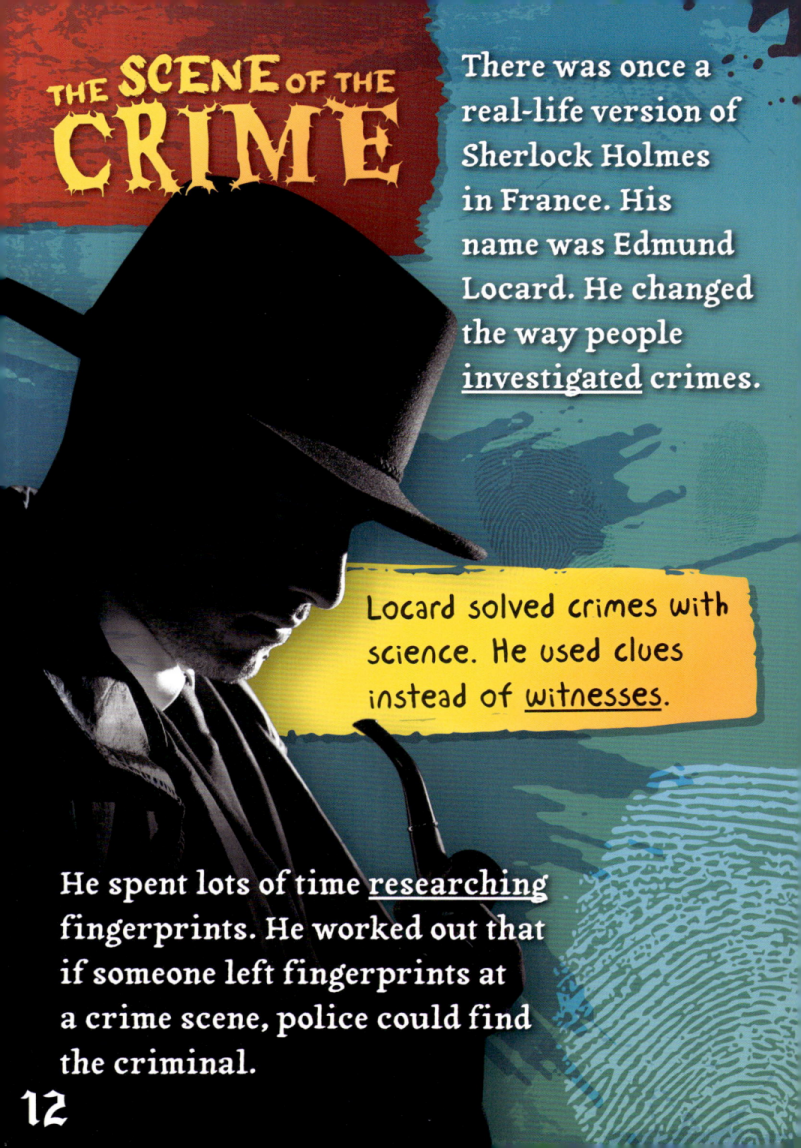

Locard also worked out that things such as makeup and hairs can be passed between two people when they touch.

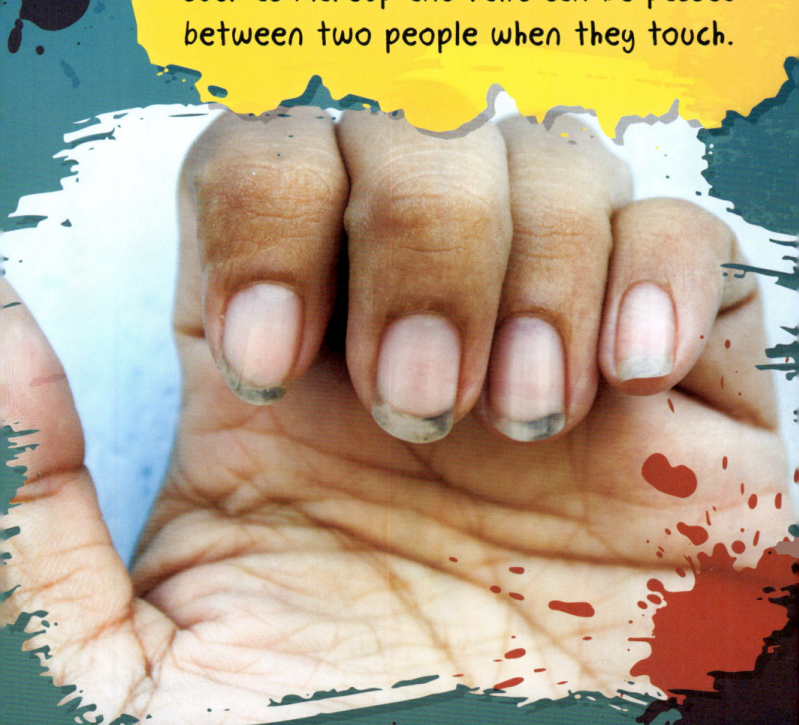

Locard used it to solve crimes. In 1912, a woman had been strangled. Edmund tested her boyfriend's fingernails. He found bits of the woman's makeup underneath them. Locard had found the killer!

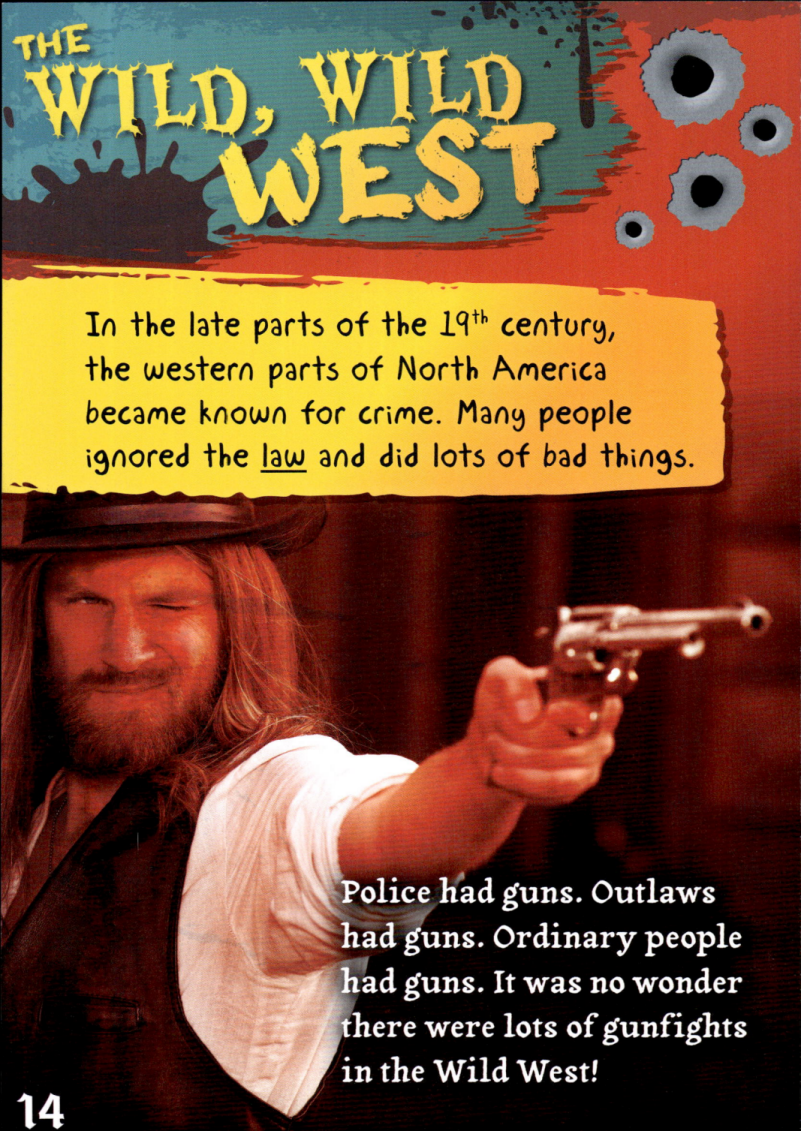

A famous group of outlaws were called the Wild Bunch. They were led by Butch Cassidy. They made money by robbing trains and banks.

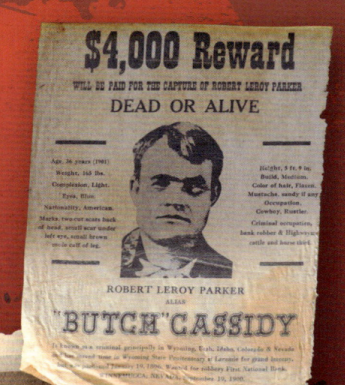

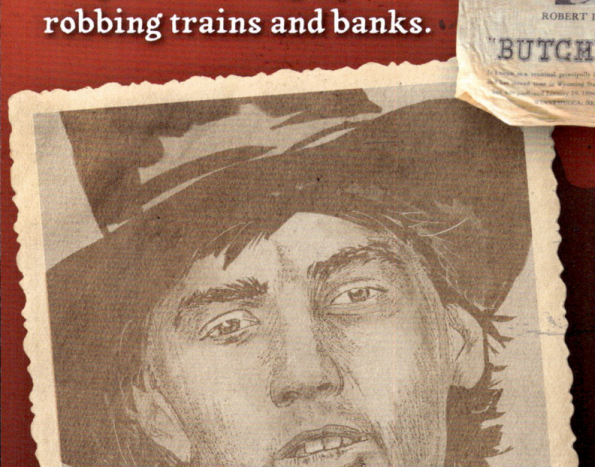

Billy the Kid was one of the most well-known gunmen in the Wild West. He was once captured by police, but he escaped and went on the run. He was finally caught and shot.

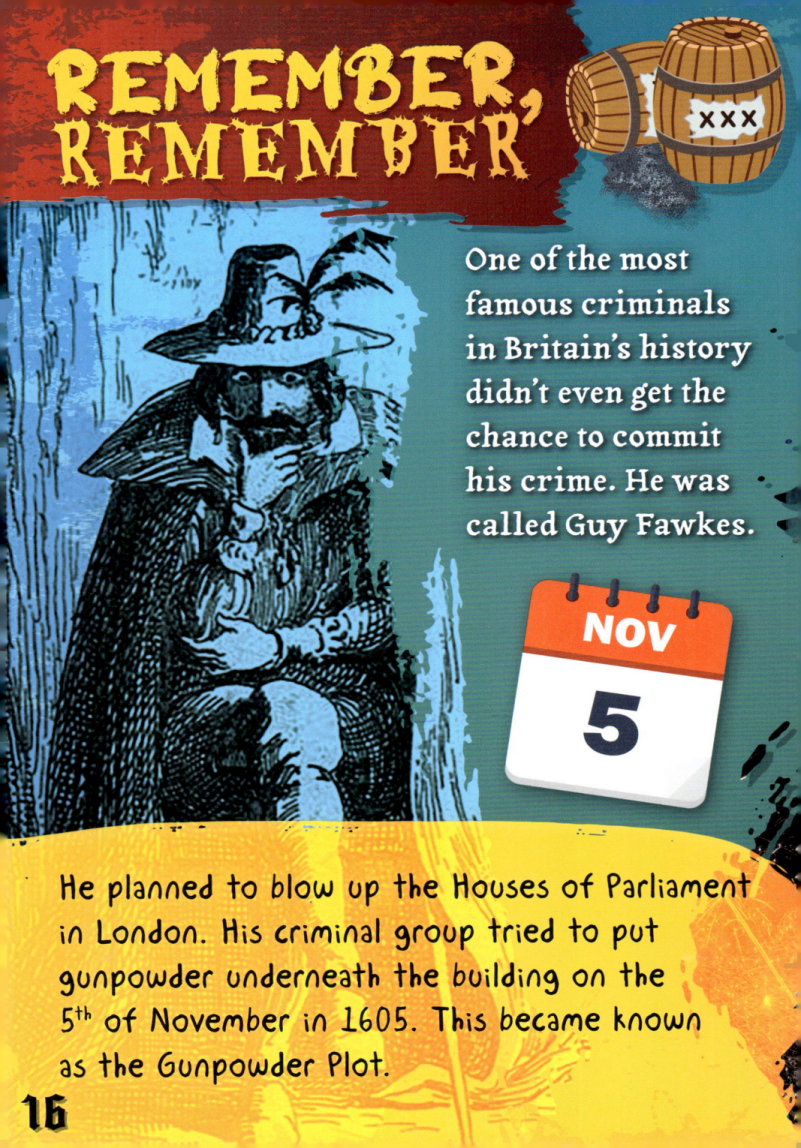

However, someone caused the plan to fail. They sent a letter to the government and Royal Family about the plan. Guy Fawkes was arrested, taken away and killed in a gruesome way!

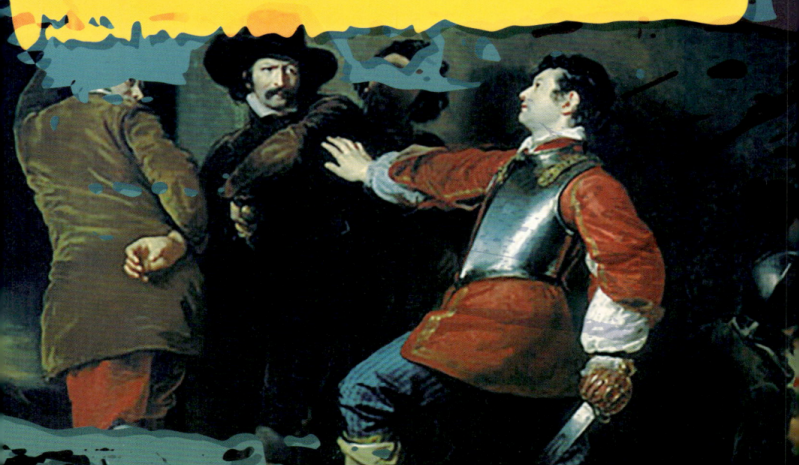

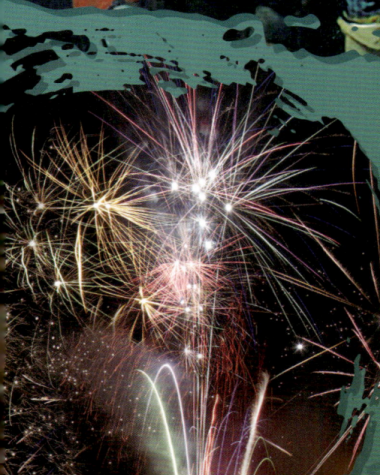

The Gunpowder Plot is remembered every year on the 5th of November in Britain. People light big fires and set off fireworks.

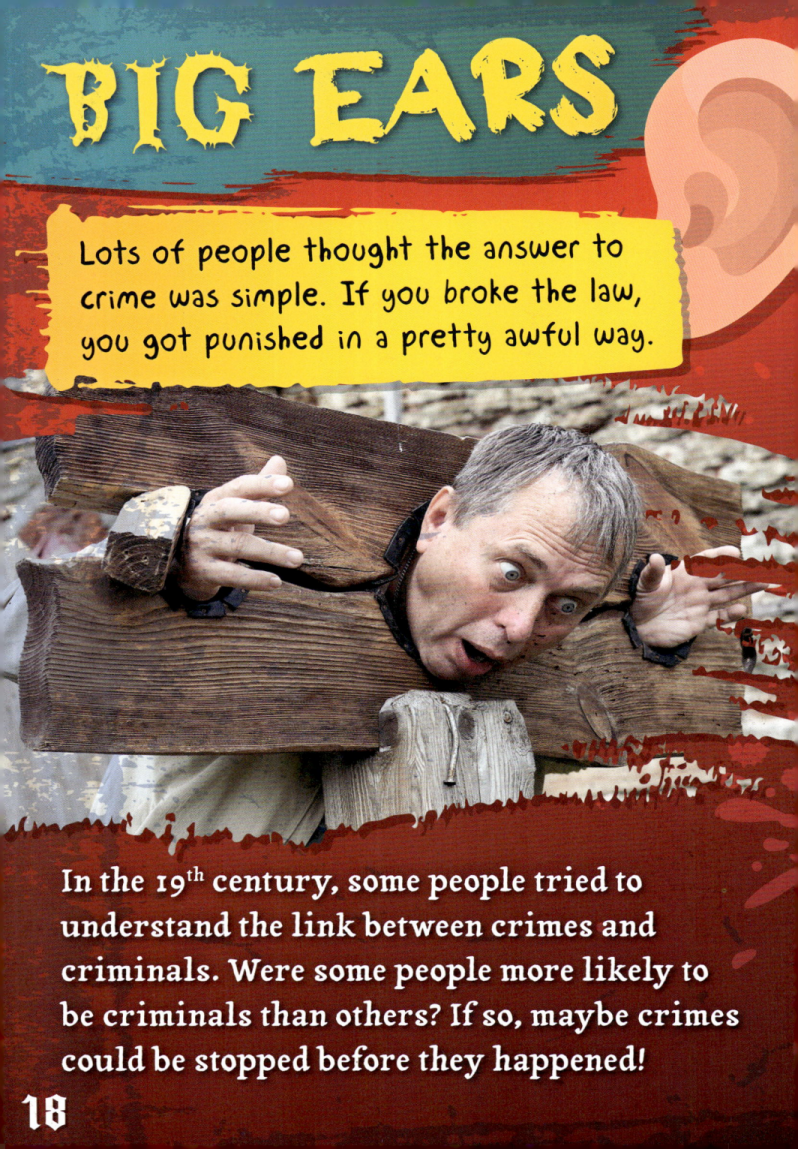

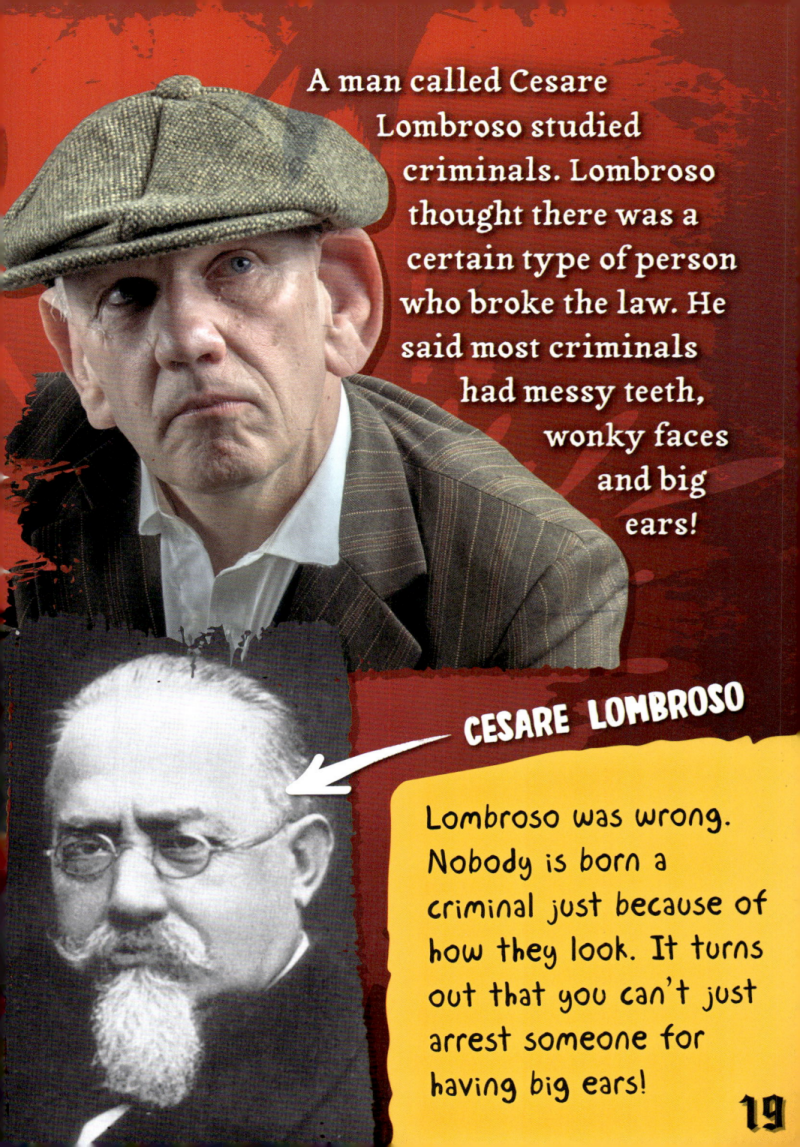

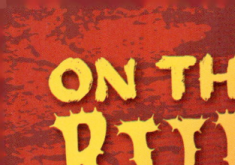

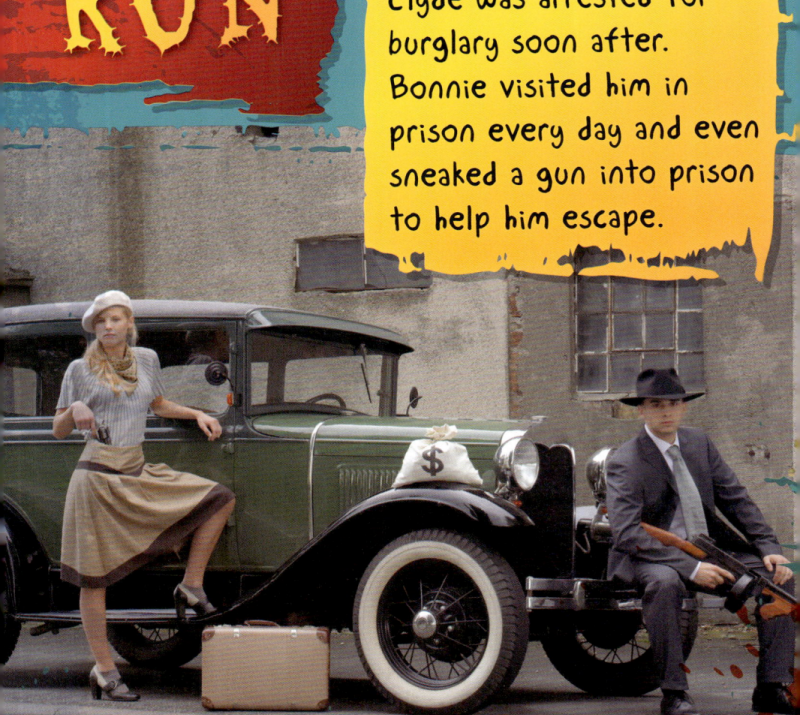

Bonnie and Clyde met in 1930 and fell in love. Clyde was arrested for burglary soon after. Bonnie visited him in prison every day and even sneaked a gun into prison to help him escape.

Bonnie and Clyde ran away together. For two years, the couple joined gangs to rob banks. They killed anyone who got in their way.

Life on the run isn't as exciting as it might sound. Bonnie and Clyde took baths in rivers and ate food from cans. They were always on the lookout to make sure they weren't caught.

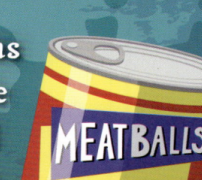

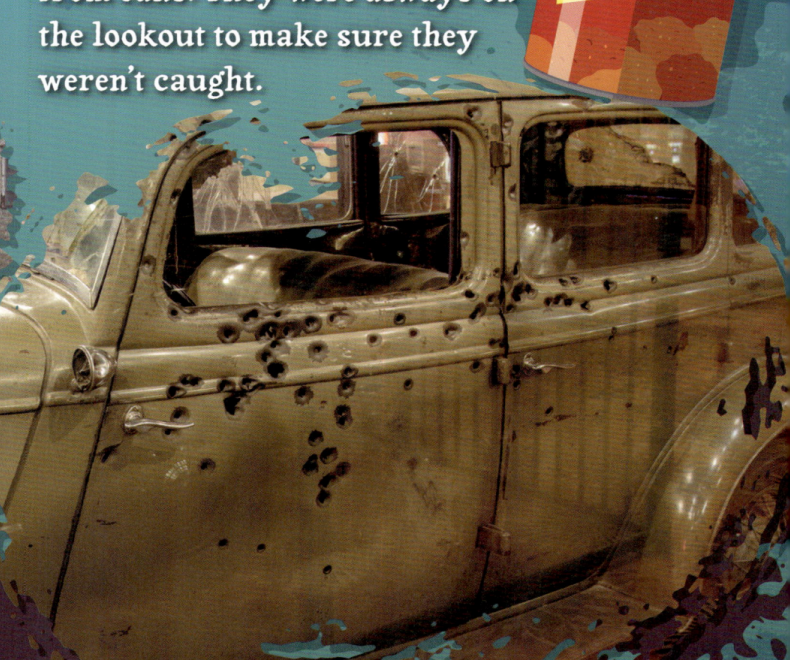

Bonnie and Clyde were killed in 1934. Police caught them visiting a friend. They fired lots of guns at the couple's car and shot them.

ROMAN RULES

Ancient Rome was not the nicest place. Wee and poo rained down from windows. Rich people had slaves. At night, people might have been attacked and had their money stolen. Would you want to live there?

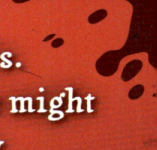

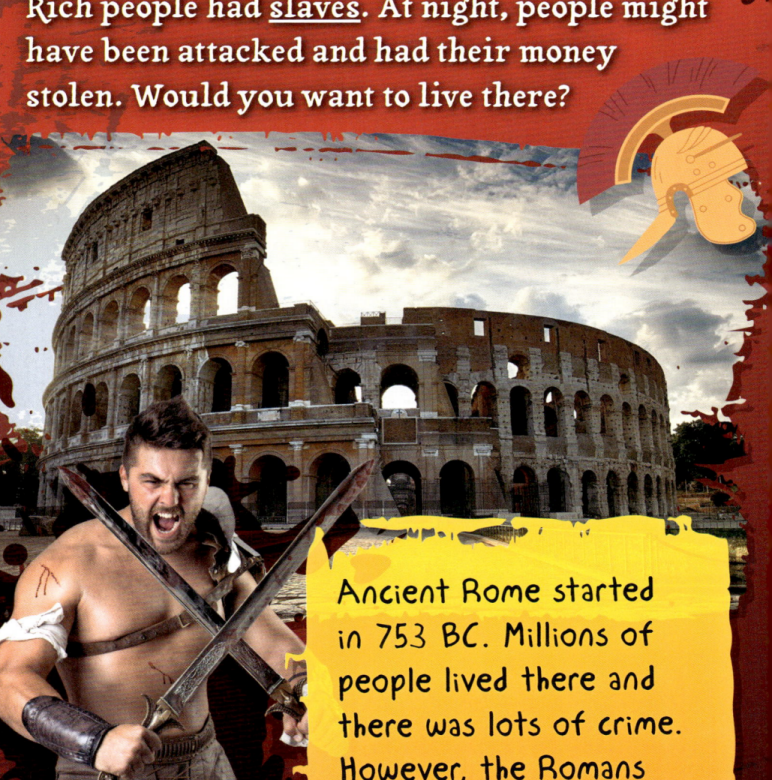

Ancient Rome started in 753 BC. Millions of people lived there and there was lots of crime. However, the Romans didn't have a police force!

Instead, they had people called vigiles. They usually tried to stop fires, but they also looked out for crime. Some vigiles were good people. Others were not so good.

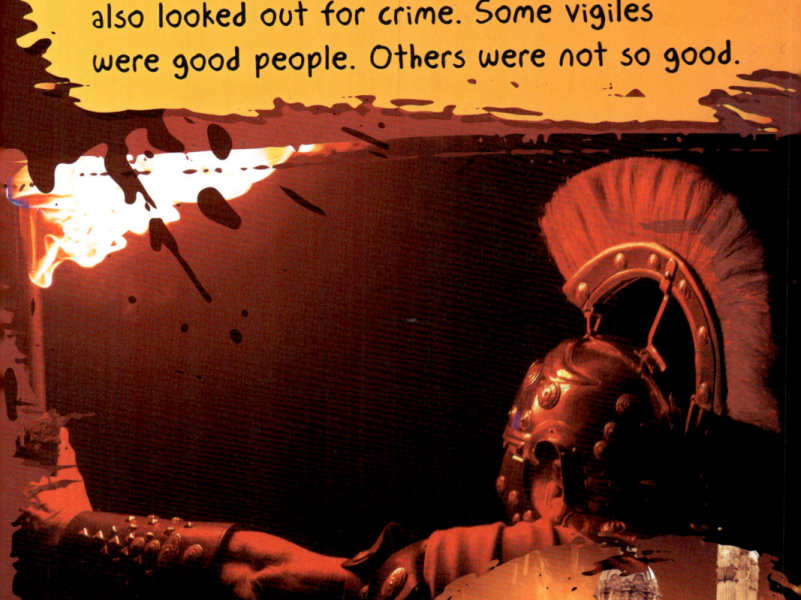

There are stories of vigiles committing crimes themselves. Some vigiles once went around the city stealing while there was a huge fire!

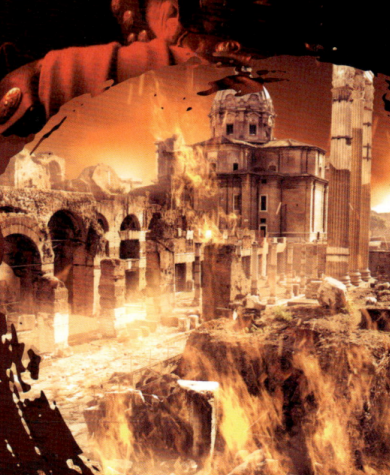

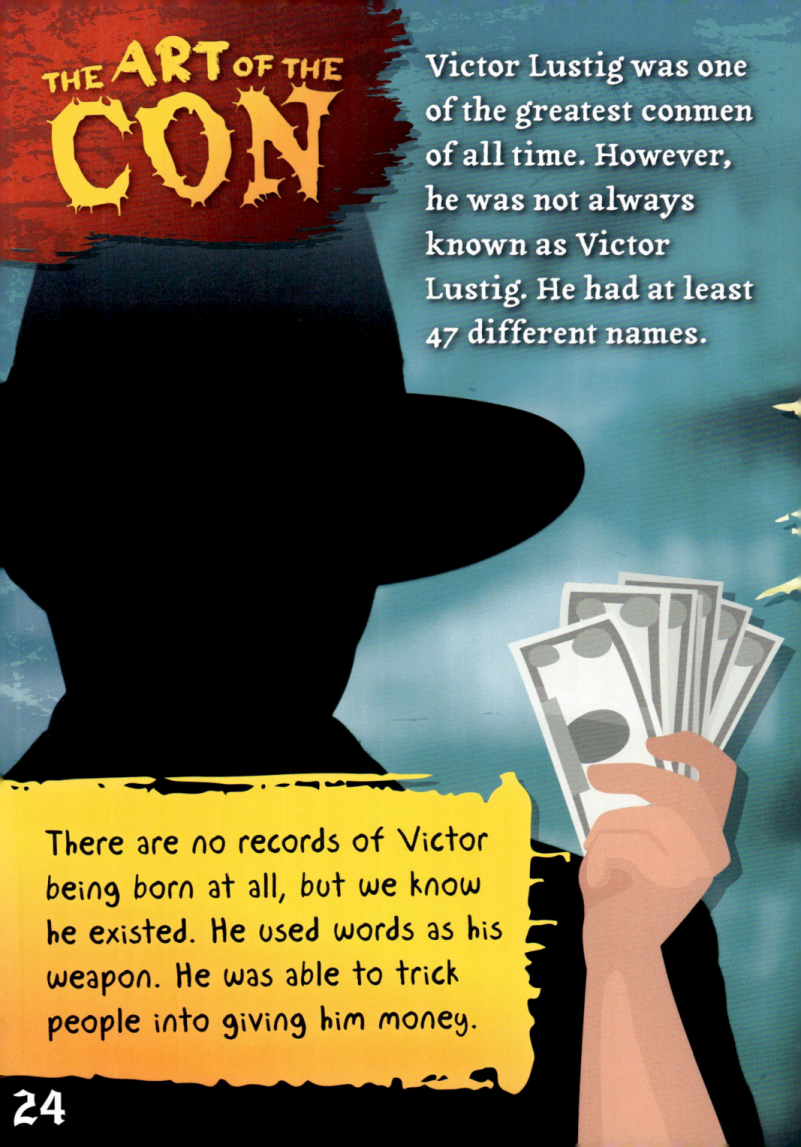

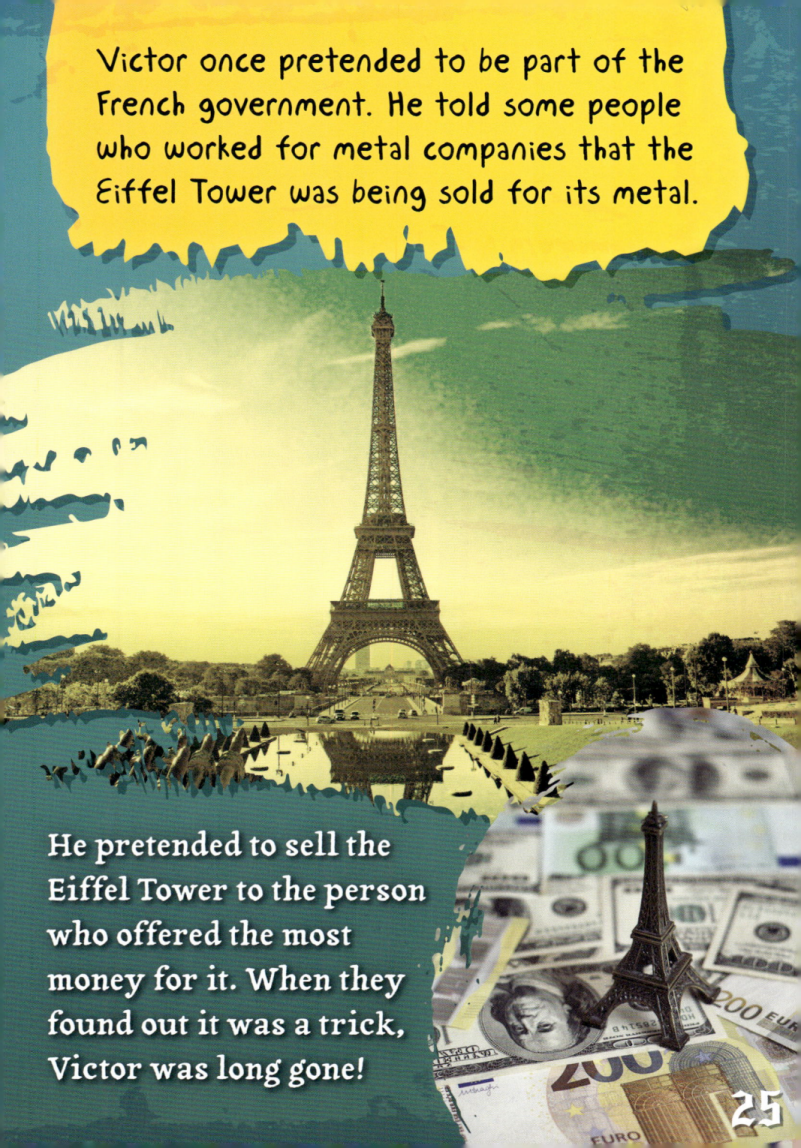

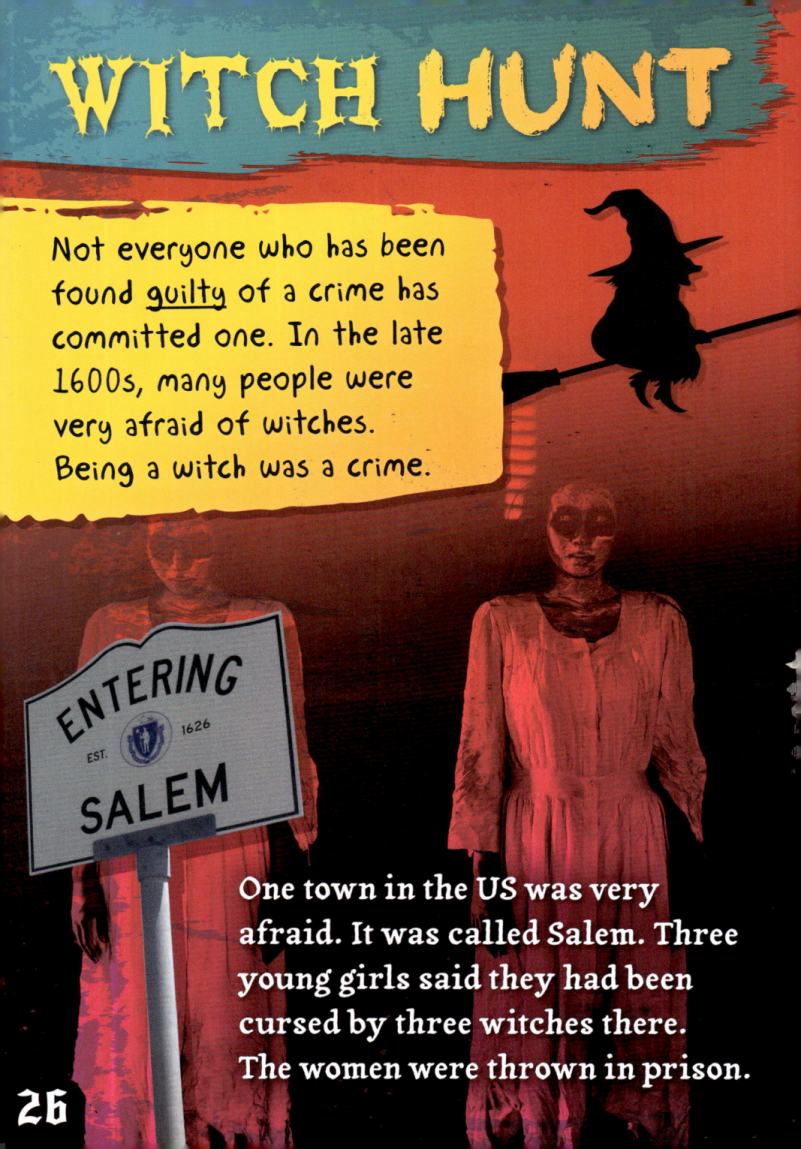

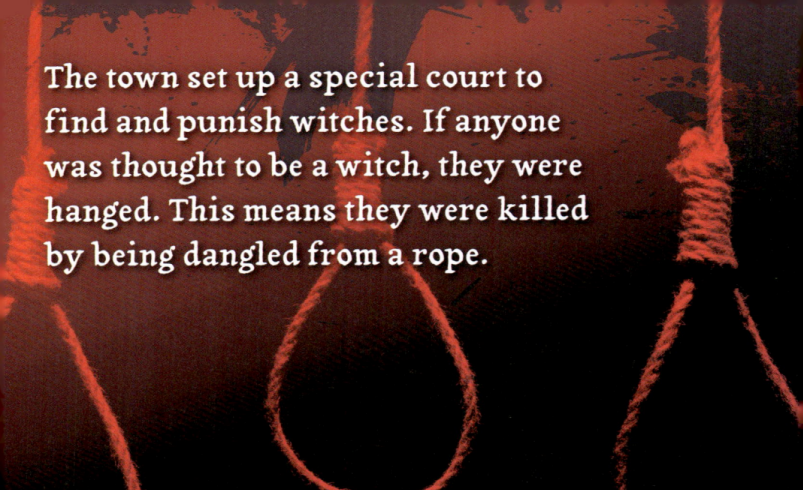

The town set up a special court to find and punish witches. If anyone was thought to be a witch, they were hanged. This means they were killed by being dangled from a rope.

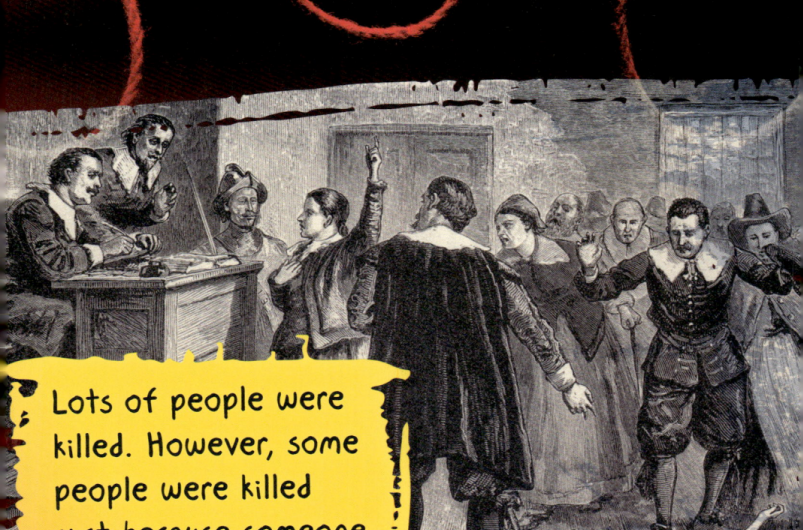

Lots of people were killed. However, some people were killed just because someone else dreamt they were a witch! How hideous!

TERRIBLE TORTURE

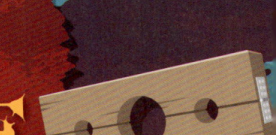

Today, lots of different things stop people committing crimes. These include police, cameras and alarms. None of these things existed far back in the past.

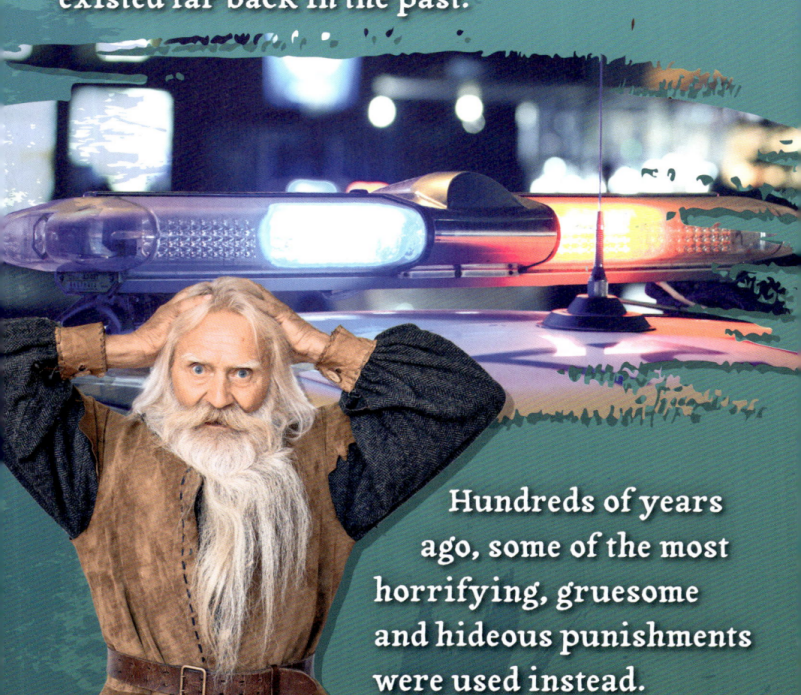

Hundreds of years ago, some of the most horrifying, gruesome and hideous punishments were used instead.

RED HOT

People might have been asked to hold a red-hot iron bar. If their hands healed after three days, they were not guilty.

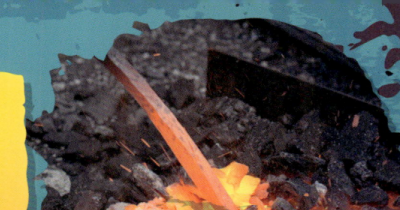

CRACK THAT WHIP

People were whipped on the back if they didn't work hard enough.

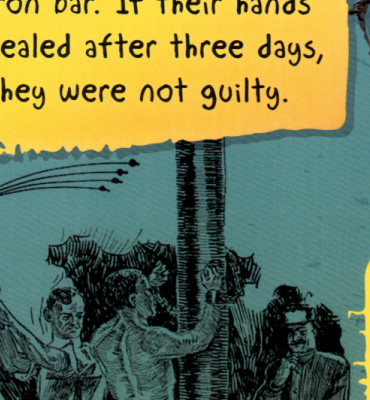

CHOP, CHOP

People were sometimes punished by having body parts cut off. Someone who was caught stealing might have had their hands chopped off.

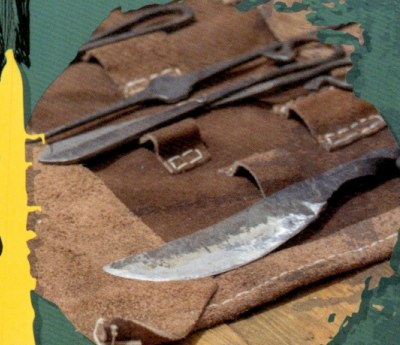

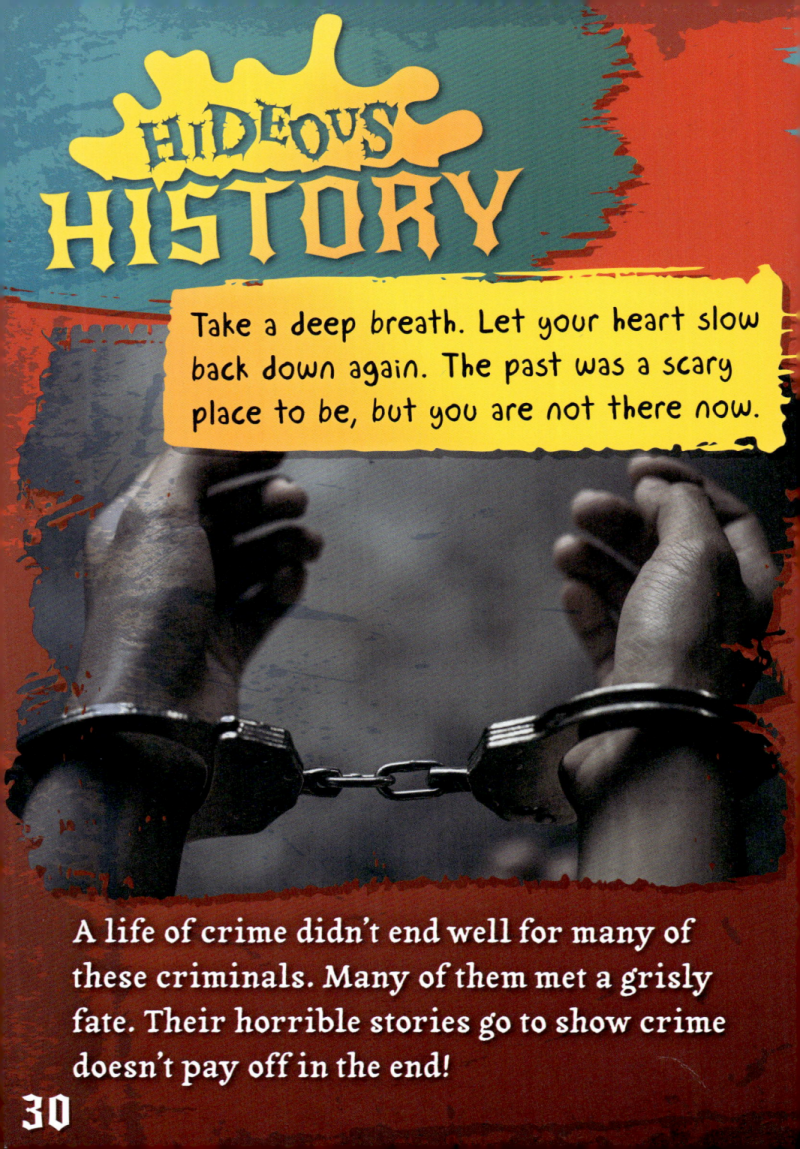

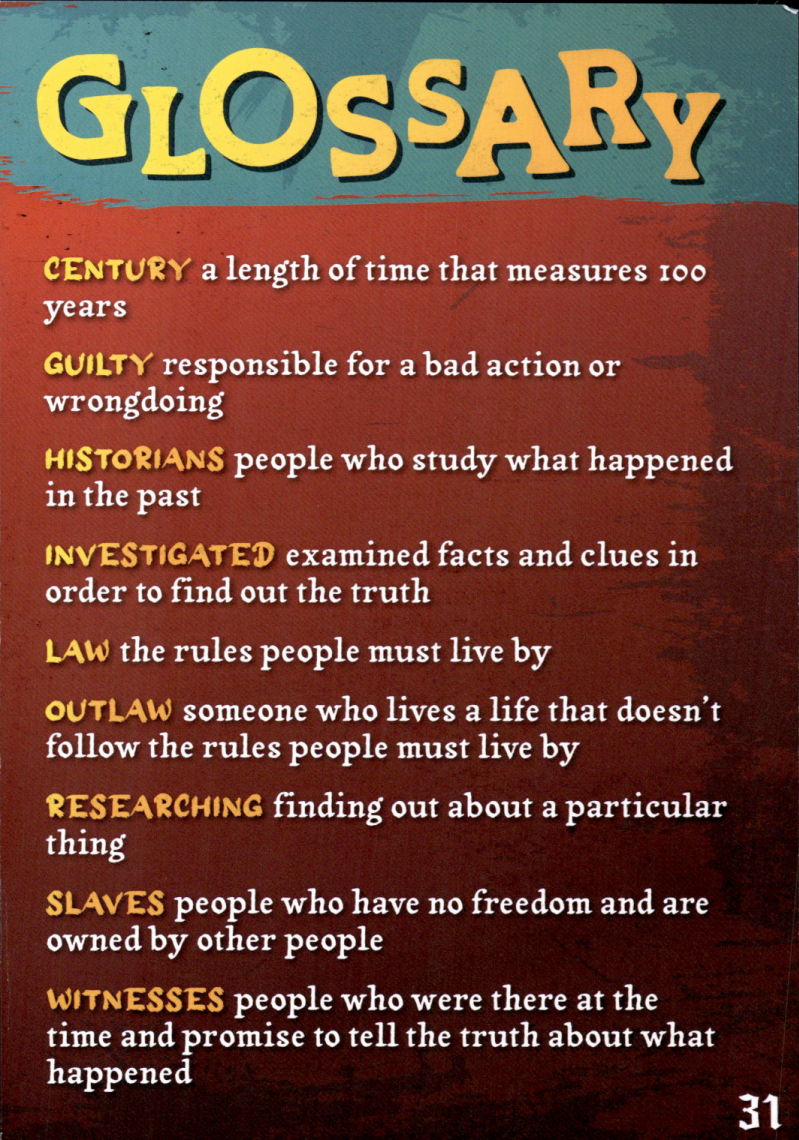

INDEX

CONMEN 24

FIRES 17, 23

GUNS 14–15, 20–21

LAWS 14, 18–19

OUTLAWS 10–11, 14–15

PIRATES 6

POLICE 9, 12, 14–15, 21–22, 28

PUNISHMENTS 5, 28

STEALING 10, 23, 29

WITCHES 26–27

AN INTRODUCTION TO BOOKLIFE RAPID READERS...

Packed full of gripping topics and twisted tales, BookLife Rapid Readers are perfect for older children looking to propel their reading up to top speed. With three levels based on our planet's fastest animals, children will be able to find the perfect point from which to accelerate their reading journey. From the spooky to the silly, these roaring reads will turn every child at every reading level into a prolific page-turner!

CHEETAH

The fastest animals on land, cheetahs will be taking their first strides as they race to top speed.

MARLIN

The fastest animals under water, marlins will be blasting through their journey.

FALCON

The fastest animals in the air, falcons will be flying at top speed as they tear through the skies.

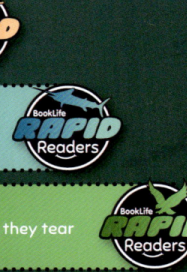